Made in the USA
Las Vegas, NV
10 August 2021

27787436R00070